Guide to
Pub Walks

Nigel Vile

The Avon Vale

COUNTRYSIDE BOOKS
NEWBURY BERKSHIRE

First published 2018
© Nigel Vile 2018

COUNTRYSIDE BOOKS
3 Catherine Road
Newbury, Berkshire

To view our complete range of books,
please visit us at
www.countrysidebooks.co.uk

ISBN 978 1 84674 358 0

Cover design by Barrie Appleby

Designed by KT Designs, St Helens
Produced through The Letterworks Ltd., Reading
Typeset by KT Designs, St Helens
Printed in Poland

Introduction

What better way to spend a leisurely few hours than to stretch your legs and then visit a traditional pub for a delicious meal and a glass of beer or wine? The 20 circular walks in this book allow you to do just that. Each route – which includes, or is just a short drive from, a recommended pub – takes you through some of the finest scenery in Wiltshire.

There is the well-known chalk downland, rising to almost 1,000 feet above sea level at Tan Hill, east of Devizes. Below the chalk hills lie the clay vales, rich dairying pastures and arable land that border rivers like the Wylye, the Kennet and the Avon. Many of Britain's most famous prehistoric remains are here: vast stone circles at Stonehenge and Avebury; West Kennett, with its famed long barrow; and a white horse from the 1600s gleaming on the chalk hillside above Bratton and Westbury.

The Red Lion, Avebury

There are also the stunning villages and towns, carved from the glorious local bedrock – Castle Combe, for example, and Bradford-on-Avon. Add the great landed estates at Longleat and Stourhead, as well as the upper reaches of the Thames at Cricklade and the glorious hanging valleys on Cranborne Chase, and you have as delightful a series of landscape types as you could wish to enjoy.

The walks are between two and seven miles in length. Car parking options in the vicinity of each pub have been suggested, although in many cases it will be possible to park at the hostelry itself. In such cases, you must seek the permission of the pub in case parking is at a premium, and promise to return for a meal and a drink. A sketch map indicating the route to be followed accompanies each walk. However, I would always recommend carrying the relevant OS Explorer map as well – these are as vital a part of the walker's kit as sturdy boots and a rucksack. The appropriate sheet number is given at the start of each walk.

To make your day complete, do not forget to carry a snack and a drink in that trusty rucksack, as well as a decent set of waterproofs. Despite occasional belief to the contrary, authors of walking guidebooks cannot guarantee their readers sunny weather!

Nigel Vile

Publisher's Note
We hope that you obtain considerable enjoyment from this book; great care has been taken in its preparation. However, changes of landlord and actual pub closures are sadly not uncommon. Likewise, although at the time of publication all routes followed public rights of way or permitted paths, diversion orders can be made and permissions withdrawn.

We cannot, of course, be held responsible for such diversion orders or any inaccuracies in the text which result from these or any other changes to the routes, nor any damage which might result from walkers trespassing on private property. We are anxious, though, that all details covering the walks and the pubs are kept up to date, and would therefore welcome information from readers which would be relevant to future editions.

To get in touch visit our website: www.countrysidebooks.co.uk

The roundhouse

1 Cricklade
5½ miles (8.9 km)

WALK HIGHLIGHTS
The Saxon settlement of Cricklade is the first town on the River Thames. From the High Street, with its handsome 17th- and 18th-century buildings, the walk heads out to Cerney Wick along the former Midland and South Western Junction Railway, which is now a footpath and cycle route. The return is quite literally water, water, everywhere, as we explore the long-defunct Thames & Severn and Wilts & Berks Canals, before following a stretch of the infant River Thames across North Meadow, famous for fauna such as the marsh fritillary. At journey's end is the Red Lion Inn, with its very own Hop Kettle Brewery.

THE PUB
The Red Lion Inn www.theredlioncricklade.co.uk
☎ 01793 750776 **SN6 6DD**

Guide to Wiltshire Pub Walks

HOW TO GET THERE AND PARKING: Cricklade lies just off the A419 Cirencester road, seven miles north-west of Swindon. In the centre of the town, opposite the Old Bear pub, take the turning signposted to the car park and toilets. This is just a few minutes from the Red Lion Inn, which is passed near the end of the walk. **Postcode** SN6 6AA for the car park.

MAP: OS Explorer 169 Cirencester & Swindon. **Grid ref** 102939.

THE WALK

1 Leave the car park, and turn right along the **High Street**; take the second right immediately past the **Kings Head** into **Church Lane**. Walk down to the church, and turn right by the church porch down to a property called the **Gatehouse**. Turn left, and walk through a parking area to join **Bath Road**. Follow this road ahead, initially passing a school and the local fire station, to reach a junction in 350 yards. Turn right; in 40 yards, turn left into **Stones Lane**. At the next junction, turn right, and walk past the sports centre. Immediately past the sports centre, turn left into a recreation ground. Then turn right onto a path: this is the former railway line, now Route 45 of the National Cycle Network. Follow this path for ¾ mile to a point where it crosses the infant **River Thames**. In another 350 yards, turn left at a junction to follow the signposted **Thames Path**.

2 Keep on this path – it soon bears right – to reach a junction in 150 yards. Ignoring the **Thames Path** on the left, follow the footpath ahead for ½ mile to a road. Turn right, and follow this road over the railway path and on into **Cerney Wick**. Follow the road as it winds its way through the village, ignoring one turning, to reach a junction by the **Crown Inn**. Turn right – signposted to **Down Ampney** and **Cricklade** – to reach the **Thames & Severn Canal** in 150 yards. Turn right, and follow the towpath alongside the canal bed, signposted to **Cricklade**. In ¾ mile, pass **Latton Basin**, which marks the junction with the **Wilts & Berks Canal**, to reach a gate and a track. Turn right, keeping to the track as it bears right down to the entrance to **Basin Cottage**. Follow the path that runs to the left of this property down to the towpath of the **Wilts & Berks Canal**. Follow this towpath for 350 yards to a footbridge over a stream, before following the disused canal for 150 yards to a bridge over the **Thames**.

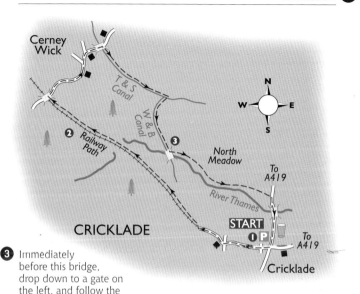

3 Immediately before this bridge, drop down to a gate on the left, and follow the **Thames** downstream as it runs alongside **North Meadow**. In 300 yards, by a footbridge and an information board, veer left to continue along the edge of **North Meadow** until the next information board and footbridge. Ignoring this turning, continue across **North Meadow**, shortly passing a telegraph pole on the left, to reach the next junction by the **Thames** in 350 yards. At this point, veer right to cross the river, before following a path into a field and across to a stile by **High Bridge**. Turn right, and follow the road into **Cricklade**, passing the **Red Lion Inn** as you enter the town. In another 200 yards, opposite the **Old Bear** pub, turn right to find the car park.

PLACES OF INTEREST NEARBY

The **Swindon and Cricklade Railway** (www.swindon-cricklade-railway. org) is at nearby Blunsdon.

The Smoking Dog pub

2 Malmesbury

2½ miles (4 km)

WALK HIGHLIGHTS

Alfred the Great granted Malmesbury a charter in around AD 880, making it England's oldest borough. History is everywhere in the town; the ancient abbey is but the jewel in the crown. Also lying along the way on this walk are the market cross, dating from 1490; almshouses dating from the 17th century; and a four-storey former cloth mill. The mill is a reminder that Malmesbury was once a thriving weaving centre, with the River Avon powering the local waterwheels. Malmesbury marks the confluence of two of the Avon's tributaries, known as the Tetbury Branch and the Sherston Branch. This is a delightful waterside walk, with the riverbank sections providing a marked contrast with the town sections of the walk.

THE PUB

The Smoking Dog www.butcombe.com/pubs/the-smoking-dog
☎ 01666 825823 **SN16 9AT**

HOW TO GET THERE AND PARKING: Malmesbury lies ten miles north of Chippenham on the A429 Cirencester road. Approaching the town from the south, leave the A429 at the first roundabout to follow the 'Town Centre' turning. This road crosses the Avon at St John's Bridge; the Smoking Dog is 200 yards further on, at the lower end of the High Street. There is no car park at the Smoking Dog, with parking on the roadside opposite permitted for just one hour (Sundays excepted). 150 metres south of the pub, parking is permitted in St John's Street alongside the Rose & Crown for up to 23 hours. This should provide ample time to complete the walk! **Postcode** SN16 9BN for St John's Street.

MAP: OS Explorer 168 Stroud, Tetbury & Malmesbury. **Grid ref** 934870.

THE WALK

1 Continue along **St John's Street**, walking away from the B4042. In 200 yards, having crossed the **River Avon**, turn left immediately past the local bowls club; follow a path along to a bridge over the Avon and a stile. Follow the footpath ahead for 350 yards to the B4040 and a bridge over the Avon. Cross this bridge, and immediately turn left – ahead is an Indian restaurant called the **Spice Merchant** – to follow a path alongside the Avon through the **Conygre Mead Nature Reserve**. In 250 yards, the path passes through a gateway to emerge into a parking area.

2 Turn left, cross the river, and follow a path uphill towards **Malmesbury**'s town centre. At an early junction, climb the steps ahead, and keep on the stepped path as it bears left to emerge in 200 yards by the **Whole Hog** restaurant and Malmesbury's market cross. Turn sharply right, and pass through an archway into the abbey's churchyard. Walk straight ahead to the abbey's main entrance, before bearing left to leave the churchyard by the **Old Bell Hotel**. Follow **Gloucester Street** ahead, shortly passing **Abbey Row** on the right, to reach the **Triangle**. Bear left into **Bristol Street**; after 175 yards, bear left into **Foxley Road**. Keep on **Foxley Road** as it bears left to cross the **Avon**, before following a track on the left to a stile on the left.

3 Beyond the stile, follow a path across meadowland bordering the **Avon**

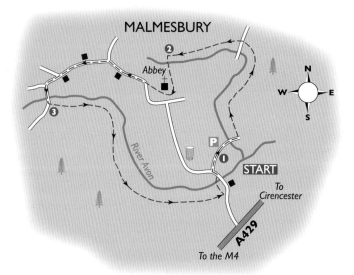

for 200 yards; you will reach a stone footbridge over the **Avon** on the left. Ignoring this bridge, follow the river downstream for 200 yards, before veering right across to a gap in the hedgerow. Beyond this gap, turn left to a handgate before following the path ahead for 600 yards, passing through gates bordering the **Avon** for most of the way, to emerge onto the B4014 by **Avon Mills**. Turn left; in 100 yards, the first right by the **Rose & Crown** is St John's Street. For the **Smoking Dog**. continue up the **High Street** for 200 yards; the pub is on the right-hand side of the road.

PLACES OF INTEREST NEARBY

Malmesbury's **Abbey House Gardens** (www.abbeyhousegardens. co.uk) is home to over 10,000 different plants. The first King of England is buried somewhere in its five acres and two saints were thrown down its well. **SN16 9AS**

Approaching Sherston

3 Sherston

6 miles (9.7 km)

WALK HIGHLIGHTS

Sherston, Luckington and Sopworth lie in the southern fringes of the Cotswolds. Although set some distance from the heart of this much-loved landscape, this walk's picturesque limestone cottages, ancient churches, sparkling rivers and gently undulating pasture all combine to give the route a real Cotswold feel. Sherston's wide main street tells of its medieval status as a borough with a regular market, whilst Luckington Court is familiar from a BBC production of *Pride and Prejudice*. The walk also features an infant River Avon, a far cry from the river that we find in Bristol's bustling city centre.

THE PUB

The Rattlebone Inn www.therattlebone.co.uk
☎ 01666 840871 **SN16 0LR**

THE WALK

1 Facing the **Rattlebone Inn**, turn right along **Sherston High Street**; then walk downhill on **Brook Hill**. Having crossed the infant **Avon**, pass

11

Guide to Wiltshire Pub Walks

HOW TO GET THERE AND PARKING: Sherston lies on the B4040, midway between Acton Turville and Malmesbury. There is roadside parking by Holy Cross Church, almost opposite the Rattlebone Inn. **Postcode** SN16 0LR

MAP: OS Explorer 168 Stroud, Tetbury & Malmesbury. **Grid ref** 854860.

through a handgate on the left, bear right, and walk across a meadow to a footbridge. Bear right to a handgate; enter **Grove Wood**. Follow the path to the right for 200 yards to arrive at a gate at the end of the wood. Keep on the path as it veers left and climbs uphill; it arrives at a stone slab stile on the left at the top of the field. Cross the next field to a stile and a lane; turn right to reach a ford in **Brook End** in ½ mile. Cross the bridge alongside the ford to reach a crossroads, before turning left to follow a cul-de-sac lane past a number of properties. Where the road ends, continue along a raised pavement alongside a stream. Keep to the path – it shortly bears right – and continue up to **Luckington Church**. Enter the churchyard, walk around to the far side of the church, and follow the access drive ahead to a road. Turn right, and walk up to **Luckington village green**.

❷ Follow the road to the right of the green up to the B4040; then take the road opposite (**Sopworth Road**). In 300 yards, by the speed limit signs on the edge of the village, pass through a gateway on the left; walk up some steps into a field. Bear half-right across this field to a stile in the middle of the bottom boundary; cross the next field to a gap opposite by an oak tree. Follow the right-hand edge of the next field to a stile and a driveway. Follow this driveway to the left to **Wick Farm**, before bearing right and walking down towards **Luckley Farm**. Where the road bears left to **Luckley Farm**, pass through a gateway ahead; walk downhill to a small footbridge over a seasonal stream; then climb uphill to a farm gate. Walk across to the far-right corner of the next field, join **Sopworth Road**, and follow it to the left into **Sopworth**; walk ahead at a crossroads after 300 yards.

❸ Where the road bears left in **Sopworth**, follow an enclosed footpath ahead up to the village church. Turn right in the churchyard towards a gate; go through, and cross the right-hand edge of a field to a stile. Walk the length of another long field to a gate and a stile – ignore the gate to their left – before walking straight across

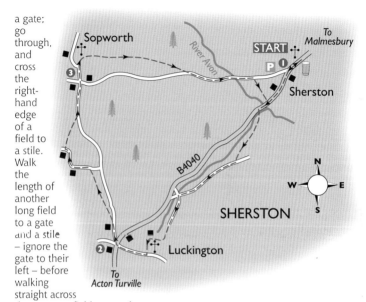

the next two fields to reach a stone footbridge. Beyond this bridge, walk straight ahead to a gate by **Stan Bridge**, join a lane, and turn left. In 600 yards, cross a stile on the right opposite **Hillberry Lodge**; follow a footpath across a hilltop known as 'the Cliff'. In 300 yards, cross a stile; then follow an access road past the fronts of a number of properties – the first of which is **Silk Mill Cottage** – back to the B4040. Turn left, and follow this road back up **Brook Hill** and along the **High Street** to the **Rattlebone Inn**.

PLACES OF INTEREST NEARBY
Sherston Wine Company, established in 1975, is opposite Holy Cross Church.

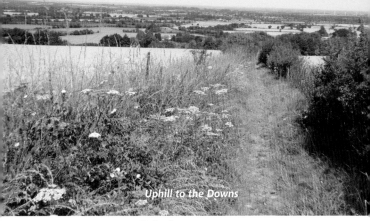

Uphill to the Downs

4 Bishopstone

6 miles (9.7 km)

WALK HIGHLIGHTS

Bishopstone is everything a village should be. There is a school overlooking the village pond, a number of thatched cottages and a traditional village pub. There is also the Church of St Mary the Virgin, where an ornate late Norman doorway in the chancel caught the eye of Nikolaus Pevsner. Helen Browning, whose organic brands are distributed nationwide, farms in the village, and her fine products can be sampled at the Royal Oak. Field paths take the walk to neighbouring Idstone and Ashbury; there is then a climb up onto the Ridgeway, Britain's oldest road. All around lies traditional Wiltshire downland, with ancient field systems and strip lynchets testifying to the long history of human settlement in the area.

THE PUB

The Royal Oak www.helenbrowningsorganic.co.uk/royal-oak
☎ 01793 790481 **SN6 8PP**

THE WALK

1 Facing the pond, follow the main road to the left before taking an early

HOW TO GET THERE AND PARKING: The B4000 runs from Shrivenham to Lambourn. Leave this road at Ashbury to follow an unclassified road into Bishopstone. Park on the roadside in the vicinity of the village pond, less than a minute's walk from the Royal Oak. **Postcode** SN6 8PP

MAP: OS Explorer 170 The Vales of the White Horse. **Grid ref** 246836.

left turn into **Cues Lane**; shortly, you will pass the **Royal Oak**. Follow the road around a right-hand bend and then left in front of **Wincie Cottage**. Keep right at the next bend, by **Helen Browning's Organic Farm**, to reach a junction. Turn left along the **The Forty**; in 200 yards, just past a Thames Water property, turn right into **New Town Lane**. In

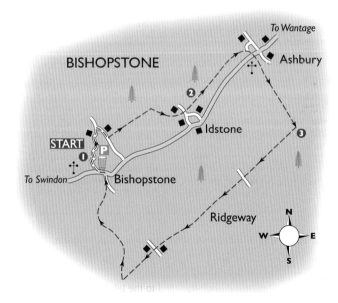

150 yards, turn left onto a path signposted to Idstone. In ¼ mile, pass through a gateway, and follow the right-hand edge of the field ahead to gates and a footbridge in its corner. In the next field, bear right, and follow the left-hand field boundary. Near the top of the field, bear left to a gate and a stile, before following a path alongside **Lower Idstone Farm** to a road. Follow the path opposite, signposted to **Ashbury**.

2 Where the enclosed path running alongside horse paddocks ends, cross a footbridge, and follow the right-hand edges of two fields to reach a track. Cross this track to a stile which is opposite and slightly to the right; then follow the left-hand edge of a field towards **Ashbury village**. In the corner of the field, pass through a gateway, and follow an enclosed path ahead between properties to reach a road junction in **Ashbury**. In front of a thatched cottage, turn right up **Chapel Lane** to arrive at a road junction and the village war memorial. Turn left; then, immediately before the **Rose & Crown Inn**, turn right along a cul-de-sac (**Church Lane**). After 100 yards, walk through the churchyard, passing to the right of the church. At the end of the churchyard, bear right down to a path, and walk ahead a few paces to a junction. Follow the path to the left, bearing left to arrive at a junction after 25 yards. Turn right, and follow an enclosed grassy path for ½ mile up to the **Ridgeway**.

3 Turn right, and follow the **Ridgeway** for 1½ miles to a junction by **Ridgeway Farm**, where the right-turn is signposted to **Bishopstone**. (Ignore other right turns along the way.) Continue along the **Ridgeway** for another ¼ mile before turning right onto a bridleway signposted to **Bishopstone**. Follow a path downhill through a valley for 350 yards to a gateway. Continue downhill through the valley – it is now much wider – for ¼ mile to the next gateway. Follow the path ahead for 350 yards, bearing slightly right, to reach **Nell Hill** in **Bishopstone**. Turn left; then turn left again at the junction to reach the pond 100 yards down the hill. Immediately before the pond are **Cues Lane** and the pub.

PLACES OF INTEREST NEARBY
Uffington Castle, the nearby **White Horse** and **Dragon Hill** all lie within a 10-minute drive of Bishopstone. (www.english-heritage. org.uk/visit/places/uffington-castle-white-horse-and-dragon-hill)

The By Brook in Castle Combe

5 Ford and Castle Combe

4½ miles (7.2 km)

WALK HIGHLIGHTS

The walk starts in the Wiltshire village of Ford, where the Old Coach Road hints at the origins of the settlement. The wooded By Brook valley, with its noted trout stream, is followed to Castle Combe, where you will almost certainly feel a sense of déjà vu. This picturesque place, with its stone cottages, market cross and ancient bridge, has featured in many films, including the 1967 version of *Doctor Dolittle* and, more recently, 2011's *War Horse*. It is also the location of the White Hart, conveniently located halfway around the walk.

THE PUB

The White Hart www.whitehartcastlecombe.co.uk
☎ 01249 782295 **SN14 7HS**

THE WALK

Cross the A420, and follow the pavement opposite to the right. In 200 yards, just past **By Brook Barn**, turn left, and follow a quiet lane uphill

Guide to Wiltshire Pub Walks

HOW TO GET THERE AND PARKING: Ford lies on the A420 between Bristol and Chippenham, five miles from Chippenham itself. There is a lay-by by the A420 in the centre of Ford, opposite a former church that is now a residence. **Postcode** SN14 8RS

MAP: OS Explorer 156 Chippenham & Bradford-on-Avon. **Grid ref** 841748.

for 200 yards to a stile on the right. Cross the stile, and walk across the field ahead to a stile opposite. Turn right, and follow an enclosed path to a gate; the path then drops downhill for 200 yards to a gate on the left, just before the **By Brook** and **Long Dean**. Pass through this gateway, walk straight ahead to a wooden footbridge; then keep going, walking straight ahead across a field with the **By Brook** on the right-hand side. Keep going through the valley, straight ahead, crossing a footbridge along the way to reach a property in ¼ mile. Just past this property, cross a bridge over the **By Brook**, and turn left to walk towards a fence.

2 Just before the fence, bear right, and follow a path uphill for 150 yards to a junction with a track. Turn left, and follow a well-defined track for ¼ mile to a marker post and a faint junction of paths. Veer right, and follow a path uphill for 200 yards before entering **Parsonage Wood**. Follow the path ahead through the woodland for 600 yards to a junction at the end of the woodland; turn left; and after 20 yards, turn left again to follow a footpath that drops downhill, joining a road on the edge of **Castle Combe**. Turn left, and walk through the village, passing the **White Hart** on the left along the way, to reach a bridge that crosses the **By Brook**. In another 300 yards, just outside the village, veer right onto a footpath that climbs uphill through **Becker's Wood**.

3 In ¼ mile, on the edge of the woodland, cross a stile, and turn left along a lane. In 25 yards, cross a stile on the right, turn left, and follow a path that runs parallel to the road, arriving at an information board. Follow the path beyond this information board through woodland; you will reach a stile and a hilltop field. Follow the path ahead across the hilltop for 300 yards to arrive at a marker post; then bear right and follow the path as it drops downhill to reach a stone slab stile and a footbridge over a river. Beyond this bridge, cross a stile and walk straight ahead along the right-hand edge of a field. At the end of this field, veer right into some woodland, and follow a path through the tree cover to an open field. Walk ahead to the left corner of this field, where there is an information board; then follow a back lane down to the A420. Turn right, and retrace your steps to the lay-by opposite the former church.

PLACES OF INTEREST NEARBY

The old market town of **Corsham** lies just four miles from Ford. The town's prosperity was based upon the wool trade and quarrying, with many local properties built from the area's golden limestone. The High Street has a definite Cotswold feel; visitors will enjoy its selection of independent shops. **Corsham Court** (www.corsham-court.co.uk), a privately owned historic house, has a significant art collection and attractive gardens.

The view from the walk

6 Bremhill

4 miles (6.4 km)

WALK HIGHLIGHTS

This walk, rich in views, is a stroll through the pages of history. Bremhill Church was associated with the poet William Lisle Bowles, rector of St Martin's for nearly 50 years; his acquaintances included Wordsworth and Charles Lamb, who both came this way. Another eccentric local character was Maud Heath, a 15th-century market trader, who became so frustrated with the state of the roads in the area that she funded a pavement known as Maud Heath's Causeway. And as for the Dumb Post Inn? Its name derives from the custom by which mailmen on carrier wagons would pin letters to a post outside the pub, in the days before the advent of the Royal Mail.

THE PUB

The Dumb Post Inn (no website)
☎ 01249 813192 **SN11 9JZ**

THE WALK

1 Facing the **Dumb Post Inn**, turn left, back along to the road junction. Turn right, and in a few paces, follow a driveway to the left, waymarked

HOW TO GET THERE AND PARKING: Follow the A4 from Chippenham towards Calne. Just before Calne, take a left turn signposted to Bremhill. In 1¼ miles, at the first junction, turn left to reach the Dumb Post Inn. There is parking directly opposite the pub. **Postcode** SN11 9JZ

MAP: OS Explorer 156 Chippenham & Bradford-on-Avon. **Grid ref** 976728.

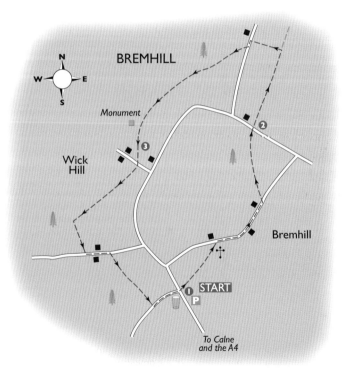

as a footpath. Beyond a gate and a stile, follow the path along the top left edges of two fields before continuing along an enclosed path to reach **Bremhill Church**. Walk around the right-hand side of the church before following a path through the churchyard and out to the road in the centre of **Bremhill**. Turn right, walking downhill out of the village; in 200 yards, at the bottom of a valley, you will reach a driveway on the left. In another 20 yards, pass through a handgate on the left, and walk across to a stile in the far-right corner of the field ahead. Walk across the next field, passing to the right of a pair of trees, to reach a stile at the top of the field. Beyond a belt of trees, cross a third field to reach a gate by a telegraph pole and a lane.

2 Cross a stile opposite; then follow the left edges of three fields. Follow the left edge of a fourth field for 200 yards to a stile on the left; cross this stile, and walk across the field ahead to a gap in the hedgerow opposite; beyond it is a lane. Turn left, and in a few paces, bear right onto a bridleway. Follow this bridleway across the right edge of a field, before continuing along a track to a second field. Continue, following the right edges of three further fields to reach **Maud Heath's monument**. Beyond this monument, continue in the same direction to a gate and a road; this is the start of **Maud Heath's Causeway**.

3 Pass through a gateway opposite, and follow the right edges of seven fields. In the seventh field, keep on the bridleway as it bears left down to a gate and a lane. Turn left, and follow the road for 350 yards to a point where a footpath crosses the road. (Ignore a slightly earlier footpath on the right, by some conifer trees.) Follow the path to the right into some woodland and down to a gate. Beyond the gate, follow the path down to another gate at the edge of the woodland. Walk across the field ahead to a gate opposite, before crossing the next field to a gate in its far-right corner. Join a lane, turn left, and walk uphill to reach the **Dumb Post Inn** in 250 yards.

PLACES OF INTEREST NEARBY

The **Calne Heritage Centre** (www.calneheritage.co.uk) offers a potted history of this fascinating corner of Wiltshire, and includes displays about the area's local celebrities.

Stone circle in Avebury

7 Avebury

6 miles (9.7 km)

WALK HIGHLIGHTS

World Heritage status, awarded by UNESCO on the basis of 'outstanding universal value', is not earned lightly; in the case of Avebury, it involves 'bearing unique testimony to civilisations that have disappeared'. The Neolithic and Bronze Age sites at Avebury are many, and extend well beyond the ubiquitous stone circle with its bank and ditch: there is a fine stone avenue, any number of barrows and the mysterious mound called Silbury Hill; there is also Britain's oldest road, the Ridgeway. Avebury's setting is unique, surrounded as it is by Wiltshire's open chalk downland, an environment of wide, open spaces, with huge skies and far-ranging vistas.

THE PUB

The Red Lion www.oldenglishinns.co.uk/our-locations/the-red-lion-avebury
☎ 01672 539266 **SN8 1RF**

HOW TO GET THERE AND PARKING: Avebury lies a mile north of the A4 at Beckhampton, on the A4361 road to Swindon. The Red Lion is in the centre of the village, and is passed near the end of the walk, which starts at the signposted National Trust car park. Parking is free for National Trust members. **Postcode** SN8 1QT

MAP: OS Explorer 157 Marlborough & Savernake Forest. **Grid ref** 099697.

THE WALK

1 Leave the car park and turn right, following the A4361 for 25 yards; then take a bridleway opposite, signposted to **Silbury Hill**. Follow this path alongside the infant Kennet for ½ mile to a gate and a bridge over the river on the right. Do not cross this bridge; instead, continue along an enclosed path to a gate, before following the path along the bottom-right edge of a field to reach the A4. Cross the A4, and turn left through a lay-by; then pass through a gateway on the right, and follow a path signposted to **West Kennett Long Barrow**. In 200 yards, having crossed the **Kennet**, pass through a handgate, and keep on the path as it bears left to reach an oak tree and a path to the right; this path leads uphill to **West Kennett Long Barrow**. Walk uphill to the barrow, retrace your steps back downhill to the oak tree, and turn right. Continue along the bottom-left edge of a field to a gate, before following an enclosed track to reach a road.

2 Cross to a gate and a stile opposite; then follow the right-hand edge of the next field to a stile in its far-right corner. Continue along an enclosed path to a junction; turn left to walk down to a road on the edge of **East Kennett**. Turn left, cross the **Kennet**, and turn right into a field. Follow the bottom-right edge of this field to its far corner and a track; this is the **Ridgeway**. Follow this track to the left for 350 yards up to the A4, by the **Sanctuary**. Cross the A4; follow the **Ridgeway** opposite for ½ mile to a junction with a byway. Turn left, and walk about 150 yards to a beech clump surrounding a barrow and a junction.

3 Pass through a gate on the left, and follow a National Trust permissive path past further collections of barrows and on downhill to reach a gate in 150 yards. Turn right, and follow a grassy path across to a gate

and the B4003, which runs
from the A4 to **Avebury**.
Cross to a gate opposite,
turn right, and walk
along the right-hand
edge of a field
to a gate and
an enclosure
housing
the **West
Kennett
Avenue**.
Walk the
whole length
of the **Avenue** into
Avebury, pass
through a gate at
the end of the
enclosure, and
cross a road
to a gate
opposite
and a clump
of trees.
Beyond these
trees, walk through a

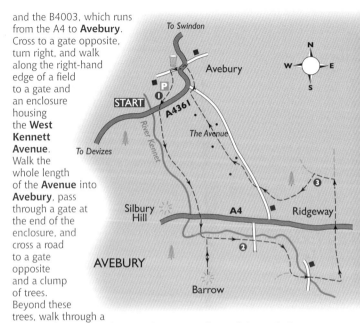

section of a stone circle to reach a gate in front of the **Red Lion**. Turn
left down the **High Street**; 25 yards beyond the **Henge Shop**, follow a
footpath on the left back to the National Trust car park.

PLACES OF INTEREST NEARBY
Avebury Manor (www.nationaltrust.org.uk/avebury) featured in
the television series *The Manor Reborn*. This showed how nine of the
manor's rooms and part of the garden were redecorated and redesigned
in five different styles: Tudor, Queen Anne, Georgian, Victorian and
20th-century.

Littlecote House

8 Ramsbury
5 miles (8 km)

WALK HIGHLIGHTS

Ramsbury's size belies its status as a village, and can be traced back to the period between 908 and 1058 when it was a thriving diocese with its own cathedral and bishop. There is still an impressive church with Anglo-Saxon origins, as well as many Jacobean and Georgian properties, all located on a fine stretch of the River Kennet. A walk through the Kennet valley brings our steps to Littlecote House, set in fine landscaped gardens and grounds; it is now a popular country house hotel. In the grounds lie the remains of Littlecote Roman Villa, with its outstanding Orpheus mosaic, whilst all around lie the rolling hills that mark the Wiltshire–Berkshire border.

THE PUB

The Bell www.thebellramsbury.com
☎ 01672 520230 **SN8 2PE**

HOW TO GET THERE AND PARKING: Ramsbury lies eight miles east of Marlborough on an unclassified road that initially passes through Mildenhall and Axford. This road is signposted from the A346 as it heads out of Marlborough towards Swindon. There is roadside parking on Ramsbury's High Street, just before the Bell. **Postcode** SN8 2PE

MAP: OS Explorers 157 Marlborough & Savernake Forest and 158 Newbury & Hungerford. **Grid ref** 276716.

THE WALK

1 Facing the **Bell**, follow the road that runs to its right, signposted to **Hungerford**. In 250 yards, take the right turn signposted to **Froxfield**. Cross the **River Kennet**; in 200 yards, take the left turn signposted to **Littlecote House**. (The turning is immediately before a red-brick property at the foot of a hill.) Shortly, at a junction by **Springshill Cottage**, walk straight ahead along a driveway. In ½ mile, the drive reaches **West Lodge**. Continue along the track for ¾ mile to a junction of paths just before a tree-lined avenue leading to **Littlecote House**. At this point, detour down the track on the left to find **Littlecote Roman Villa**.

2 For the main walk, follow the tree-lined avenue ahead; pass in front of **Littlecote House**, and walk along another tree-lined avenue to reach **East Lodge** and a road. Turn right; in 600 yards, where the road bears left by the entrance to **Littlecote House Hotel**, walk straight ahead on

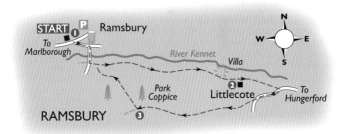

the access road leading to the manor. In 200 yards, where this access road bears right, walk straight ahead along a track. In 400 yards, at a junction by a gate, continue walking straight ahead. In just over ½ mile, at the next junction, continue for 200 yards to another junction by a **Ramsbury Park** information board.

❸ Turn right, and follow a path directly ahead uphill to some woodland. Follow the path ahead through this woodland and down to a junction in 200 yards. Follow the track ahead; in 200 yards, where the main track bears right, walk straight ahead, on the path that runs through beech woodland. In ½ mile, at a junction by **Springshill Cottage**, turn left to walk to a road. Turn right, cross the **River Kennet** in 200 yards, and continue to a junction. Turn left to arrive back at the **Square** in **Ramsbury** and the **Bell**.

PLACES OF INTEREST NEARBY
Do ensure that you take the detour to visit **Littlecote Roman Villa**. There is no website, but the Wikipedia entry contains detailed information about this amazing site.

Bradford-on-Avon

9 **Bradford-on-Avon**
4 miles (6.4 km)

WALK HIGHLIGHTS
This is a charming walk through the Avon Valley between Bradford-on-Avon – often described as 'Bath in miniature' – and Avoncliff, a canalside hamlet squeezed between the river and the Kennet and Avon Canal. The serried ranks of former weavers' cottages rise in steep tiers above the Avon in Bradford, an unforgettable sight when illuminated by the fading rays of a sunset. Avoncliff has a magnificent aqueduct that carries the canal across the Avon; it also boasts one of the finest riverside pubs in England, making this a walk 'to a pub'.

THE PUB
The Cross Guns www.crossgunsavoncliff.com
☎ 01225 862335 **BA15 2HB**

THE WALK
1 Walk to the end of the car park, drop down to the **River Avon**, and turn left under a railway bridge. Walk across a grassy recreation area to reach

29

HOW TO GET THERE AND PARKING: Bradford-on-Avon lies on the A363 road, which joins the A4 at Bathford near Bath and Trowbridge. Park in Bradford-on-Avon's railway station car park for the walk to the Cross Guns in Avoncliff. **Postcode** BA15 1EF

MAP: OS Explorer 156 Chippenham & Bradford-on-Avon. **Grid ref** 825607.

a packhorse bridge on the right. Just beyond this bridge, veer left and follow a gravel path past a tithe barn and up to the **Kennet and Avon Canal**. Follow the towpath to the right – signposted to **Avoncliff** – to reach a footbridge numbered 173 in ½ mile. Cross this bridge and turn right to follow the opposite bank of the canal along to a footbridge and a handgate. Follow the right-hand edge of the field ahead to a handgate; walk uphill in the next field, bearing left all the while, to a gate in its top-left corner.

2 Beyond the gate, follow a path through **Becky Addy Wood** to reach a lane in ¼ mile. Follow this lane to the right for 350 yards, walking downhill into **Avoncliff**; keep to the lane as it bears right just past the entrance to **Ancliff Square**. Where the lane reaches the **No. 10 Tea Gardens**, walk down some steps on the right to pass under **Avoncliff Aqueduct** and up to the **Cross Guns**; then bear right back up to the canal. Follow the towpath to the left back towards **Bradford-on-Avon**,

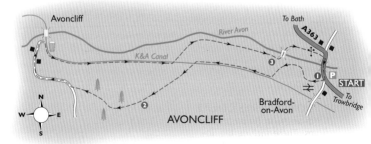

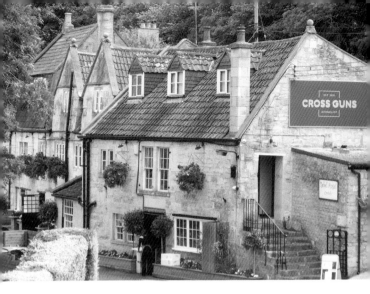

reaching bridge 173 in ¾ mile. Veer left, and follow a tarmac path down into **Barton Farm Country Park**. Follow this path for ½ mile, bordering the **Avon** and eventually arriving at the packhorse bridge passed at the start of the walk.

3 Turn left and cross the **Avon**; then take the right-hand path at a fork by the local rowing club. Cross a railway line, and follow a path through **Barton Orchard** to a junction in 250 yards, next to a property called the **Chantry**. Follow the path to the right down to the church; walk through the churchyard before crossing a bridge on the right over the **Avon**. Turn left, and follow a path along to an archway and a park alongside the **Avon** by the **Town Bridge**. Walk through the park to the A363, and turn right; in 150 yards, turn right back into the railway station car park.

PLACES OF INTEREST NEARBY
Bradford-on-Avon (www.bradfordonavon.co.uk) has many interesting attractions. These include the Town Bridge, with its lock-up; the Saxon church; the tithe barn; and St Mary Tory, a diminutive hermitage.

Seend locks

10 Seend

5½ miles (8.9 km)

WALK HIGHLIGHTS

Seend may lie just five miles west of Devizes, but on the intervening section of the Kennet and Avon Canal there are no fewer than 30 locks! The Barge Inn must prove a welcome sight to bargees. Away from the canal, this walk explores the village of Seend itself, located on a ridge formed by an outcrop of Corallian Limestone overlain by Lower Greensand. The views to the north encompass the Avon Valley, whilst to the south the outlook is across the little-known but expansive Vale of Steeple Ashton. This fine view is enjoyed by some rather grand hilltop houses, reminders of Seend's prosperous past as a weaving centre. Talking of the past, be sure to explore the village church, which has a magnificent stained-glass window dedicated to the village's history.

THE PUB

The Barge Inn www.bargeinnseend.co.uk
☎ 01380 828230 **SN12 6QB**

HOW TO GET THERE AND PARKING: Follow the A361 from Trowbridge towards Devizes. In five miles, as the A361 approaches Seend, turn left, signposted to Seend Cleeve and the Barge Inn. In ¾ mile, turn left into the Barge Inn's car park. **Postcode** SN12 6QB

MAP: OS Explorer 156 Chippenham & Bradford-on-Avon. **Grid ref** 932613.

THE WALK

1 Leave the pub car park, turn left, and cross the **Kennet and Avon Canal**. Turn left down to the towpath, turn right, and walk away from – not under – bridge 153. In a mile, cross swing bridge 155 to a gate, and follow a path across a field to a gate opposite, walking in the direction of **Seend Cleeve** on the hill ahead. Cross a second field to a gate; then follow an enclosed track for 600 yards to a gate and a junction. Turn left, and follow a track for 200 yards to arrive at the road in **Seend Cleeve**.

2 Turn left; then, at a junction in 150 yards, turn right by property number 182. Follow this side turn for ½ mile to a junction by a bench, keeping right by the entrance to **Ferrum House** along the way. Follow the road

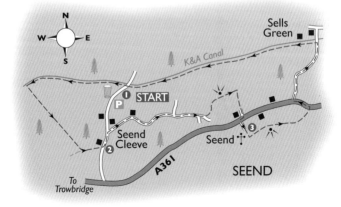

33

Guide to Wiltshire Pub Walks

The Barge Inn on the Kennet and Avon Canal

ahead, signposted to **Seend** and **Worton**. At the next junction, in 200 yards, turn left towards the school. At the following junction, by a red-brick property numbered 24, turn left and follow a track that shortly bears right to run across the hilltop; the **Avon Valley** is below on the left. In 300 yards, at a junction, turn right and walk up **Rusty Lane**, passing **Seend Community Centre** and reaching the A361. Turn right; then, in 40 yards, turn left down a lane leading to **Seend Church**. Follow the path to the left of the church down to a gate in the far-left corner of the churchyard.

3 Follow a path ahead across the hillside to a gate; there are views across the **Vale of Steeple Ashton** to your right. Continue along an enclosed path to reach some steps that drop down to a track. Cross to a stile opposite, and follow a hillside path signposted to **Inmarsh Lane**. In 300 yards, keep to the path as it bears left to reach Inmarsh Lane. Turn left up to the A361, follow the main road to the left for 200 yards before turning right into **Spout Lane**. Follow **Spout Lane** for 500 yards to a bridge that crosses the **Kennet and Avon Canal**. Cross the bridge (number 149), turn left down to the towpath, and follow the path to the right away from the bridge. Follow the canal for 1¼ miles back to bridge 153, and retrace your steps back to the **Barge Inn**.

PLACES OF INTEREST NEARBY

The nearby town of **Devizes** (www.devizes.org.uk) has much to catch the eye, including the Wadworth Brewery Visitors' Centre, a Kennet and Avon Canal Museum and the unique flight of 16 consecutive locks known as the Caen Hill Staircase.

Path to the hills

11 Pewsey
5 miles (8 km)

WALK HIGHLIGHTS
At Pewsey, the Kennet and Avon Canal is nearing the end of the 15-mile Long Pound between the Devizes and Wootton Rivers. The waterway edges its way gently along the eastern edges of the Vale of Pewsey, as if in preparation for the final climb to the summit at Crofton. To the south, the canal borders the infant River Avon, with its wetland, meadow and scrub; to the north lies Oare Hill, a fine vantage point across the Vale of Pewsey. It is a steep climb, but one that is worth every bead of perspiration once the spectacular view appears.

THE PUB
The Waterfront Bar and Bistro No website
☎ 01672 564020 **SN9 5NU**

THE WALK
1 Walk across to the canal, turn right, and follow the towpath for 1¼ miles to the second overbridge, numbered 112. Just before this bridge,

Guide to Wiltshire Pub Walks

HOW TO GET THERE AND PARKING: The pub lies on the A345 Marlborough road, ½ mile north of Pewsey. There is a public car park alongside the canal; fee payable. **Postcode** SN9 5NU

MAP: OS Explorer 157 Marlborough & Savernake Forest. **Grid ref** 158601.

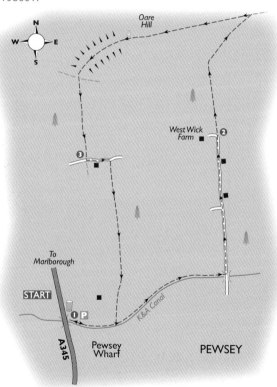

pass through a parking area on the right to reach a road. Turn left, cross the canal, and continue for ¼ mile to a junction. Ignoring the left turn to Oare, follow the cul-de-sac lane ahead, signposted to **West Wick**. Beyond some cottages, continue to a left turn to **West Wick Farm**.

2 Continue walking straight ahead to reach a gate at the foot of the downland in 600 yards. At a junction a few paces beyond this gate, bear right, and follow a footpath that climbs steeply uphill to reach a fence on the hilltop. Follow this fence to the right to reach a gate; pass through it and turn left to follow the left-hand edge of a field across the top of **Oare Hill**. At the end of the field, cross a stile, and follow the path ahead to a trig point by the **Giant's Grave**. Walk down to a gate at the bottom of the hill; then bear left to walk across a field to a gate in the bottom boundary. Cross a track into a field opposite, and follow the right-hand edge of the field down to a road.

3 Turn left, initially passing **Bethnal Cottage**, before turning right onto a track signposted to **Inlands Farm** in 200 yards. In ½ mile, where a drive on the right leads to **Inlands Farm**, walk straight ahead on a track to reach the **Kennet and Avon Canal** again. Cross a canal bridge, turn left down to the towpath, and turn left again to pass under bridge 113. Follow the towpath for 600 yards back to **Pewsey Wharf**.

PLACES OF INTEREST NEARBY

The **Pewsey Heritage Centre** (www.pewsey-heritage-centre.org.uk) documents the history of this corner of Wiltshire.

Downland escarpment

12 Heddington

5½ miles (8.9 km)

WALK HIGHLIGHTS

In 1643, Sir William Waller and his Parliamentary troops were crushed by Royalist forces at the Battle of Roundway Down during the English Civil War. The site became known as 'Runaway Hill', later corrupted to 'Roundway'. This walk explores the battlefield site, located on a vast swathe of open chalk downland. The views are pretty impressive, especially from Oliver's Castle, an ancient hillfort.

THE PUB

The Ivy Inn www.ivyinnheddington.co.uk
☎ 01380 859652 **SN11 0PL**

THE WALK

1 Facing the **Ivy Inn**, turn left, and walk up **Stockley Road** to its junction with **Church Road**. Follow **Church Road** to the left, passing the church to arrive at a junction with **Hampsley Road**. Turn right and follow this road, keeping left in front of **Church Farm**, to continue for just over ½ mile uphill to a junction by **Hill Cottage**. Turn right, and follow a very quiet hilltop lane for 350 yards to the first junction. Turn left, and follow

HOW TO GET THERE AND PARKING: Leave the A4 one mile east of Calne's town centre, and follow an unclassified road signposted to Heddington. After two miles, at a junction with Church Road just past the Ivy Inn, you will find parking for pub customers. **Postcode** SN11 0PL

MAP: OS Explorers 156 Chippenham & Bradford-on-Avon and 157 Marlborough & Savernake Forest. **Grid ref** 999662.

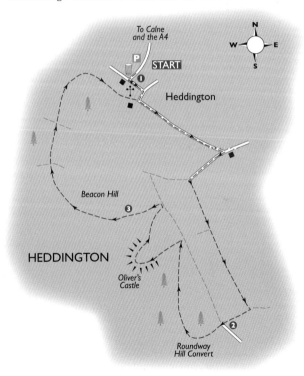

Guide to Wiltshire Pub Walks

a byway for ¼ mile to the next junction, where a byway is signposted to the right and a footpath directly ahead. Follow the footpath ahead – it runs along the left-hand edge of a field – to reach a wooden stile on the left in a little over ½ mile. Cross this stile, and follow a path to the right for a few paces before crossing another wooden stile on the right to join a track. Follow this track – soon it bears right – and continue to a parking area on the road. (This road approaches the hilltop from **Roundway village**.)

2 Pass through a handgate opposite, and follow a field path to a gateway at the entrance to **Roundway Hill Covert** (an area of woodland). In a short distance, at a junction, turn right to follow a path bordering the eastern edge of the woodland. In ½ mile, keep to this path as it bears left to a junction. Turn right, and walk a short distance to a gateway and a parking area for **Oliver's Castle**. Turn left, and in a few paces, pass through a gate on the left; now follow the path ahead out to the edge of the escarpment on **Roundway Hill**. On reaching the edge of the hilltop, bear right, and walk alongside a few trees to a post and an information board just beyond **Oliver's Castle**. Continue, walking straight ahead, and pass through a gateway on the right. Follow the path ahead for 100 yards; with another gateway ahead, bear sharply to the left and follow a path downhill through a gully to reach a gateway.

3 Follow the path ahead as it runs below the escarpment of **Beacon Hill** to a junction. Here, follow the path ahead for a few paces, before passing through a gap in the hedge on the right. Follow the enclosed path ahead for 300 yards to a crossroads of tracks; then follow the byway opposite. In 300 yards, ignore an unmetalled road on the left, walking straight ahead to reach a property on the left-hand side in 150 yards. Beyond this property, follow a track ahead through to **Church Farm** and a road in 600 yards. Turn left; then, in 100 yards, turn left at a junction back to the church and the junction with **Stockley Road**. Turn right to arrive back at the **Ivy Inn**.

PLACES OF INTEREST NEARBY

The **Atwell Wilson Motor Museum** (www.atwellwilson.org.uk) is just a few minutes away from the Ivy Inn.

40

Crofton Pumping Station

13 Wilton

4 miles (6.4 km)

WALK HIGHLIGHTS

Wilton is a small, picturesque place, the heart of the village consisting of a few brick and thatch cottages, a duck pond and the Swan Inn; it also boasts several interesting attractions that bring in large numbers of visitors each year. On a hilltop above the village stands Wilton Windmill, a five-storey brick tower mill dating from 1821. To the north of the village are the Kennet and Avon Canal and Crofton Pumping Station, whose Cornish beam engines fill the summit pound of the canal from Wilton Water. This reservoir is an attraction in its own right on account of its wildfowl, which can include pochard and teal. This is a fine walk that includes all of these attractions, together with Wilton Brail, a vast expanse of ancient woodland.

THE PUB

The Swan Inn www.theswanwilton.com
☎ 01672 870274 **SN8 3SS**

Guide to Wiltshire Pub Walks

HOW TO GET THERE AND PARKING: Wilton lies eight miles south-west of Hungerford, on a minor road that heads north from the A338. Park on the roadside in the vicinity of the Swan Inn. **Postcode** SN8 3SS

MAP: OS Explorer 157 Marlborough & Savernake Forest. **Grid ref** 268615.

THE WALK

1 At the junction opposite the **Swan**, take the left turn, signposted to **Great Bedwyn**. In 350 yards, take the second right turn, signposted to **Shalbourne** and the **Wilton Windmill**. Follow this road for ½ mile, passing **Wilton Windmill** along the way, to reach a crossroads. Turn

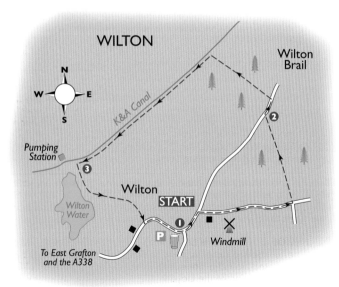

The village pond

left, and follow a track along the fringes of an area of woodland called **Bedwyn Brail** to reach a road in ½ mile.

❷ Turn right; then, in 75 yards, turn left onto a gravelled track that enters the woodland called **Wilton Brail**. In ¼ mile, where the gravelled track bears left, veer right through some bushes to a gate and an open field. Follow the path ahead across this field to reach the **Kennet and Avon Canal** by lock 163. Follow the towpath to the left for just over ¾ mile to reach **Wilton Water**, a reservoir on the left. A detour here will enable you to explore **Crofton Pumping Station**.

❸ Turn left, and follow a path that runs alongside **Wilton Water**. Enter a second field, and follow its right-hand edge to its far-right corner. Turn right down a track to the road in **Wilton** by the village pond, before turning left to arrive back at the **Swan Inn**.

PLACES OF INTEREST NEARBY

Take time to visit the stone museum in nearby **Great Bedwyn**. This museum is based around a stone masonry business founded in 1790; the seventh generation of the Lloyd family is now at the helm. (www.johnlloydofbedwyn.com)

The Westbury White Horse

14 Bratton

4 miles (6.4 km)

WALK HIGHLIGHTS

The tracks and field paths of this walk embrace some of the finest downland in southern England, together with Wiltshire's oldest white horse, an Iron Age hillfort and some most impressive views. The Westbury White Horse was remodelled in 1778, the original having been described as 'a squat ungainly creature with a reptilian tail'. Bratton Camp, with its double bank and ditch, commands fine views whose landmarks are pinpointed by a neighbouring topograph. This is a bracing upland walk for which a clear, fine day is almost obligatory.

THE PUB

The Duke www.dukebratton.cascadepubs.co.uk
☎ 01380 830242 **BA13 4RW**

THE WALK

1 With your back to the **Duke**, follow the B3098 to the right, in the direction of **Westbury**, for 250 yards; you will arrive at a minor crossroads, with

HOW TO GET THERE AND PARKING: Bratton lies three miles east of Westbury on the B3098 road. Park on the roadside – or on one of the side roads – in the vicinity of the Duke, which is in the centre of the village. **Postcode** BA13 4RW

MAP: OS Explorer 143 Warminster & Trowbridge. **Grid ref** 915524.

Court Lane on the right. At this point, turn left along the unmarked lane leading past **Turnpike Cottage**. In 200 yards, at another minor crossroads, turn right along an access lane for a number of properties. In 100 yards, where the metalled lane ends at the entrance to the last property, walk straight ahead along an enclosed track for 300 yards to reach the lane going up from **Bratton** to **Bratton Camp**. Turn left, and follow the lane uphill for 500 yards; immediately beyond a bridleway, you will reach a gate on the right. Pass through this gateway, bear left, and walk 150 yards uphill to reach a gate at the entrance to **Bratton Camp**, a hillfort.

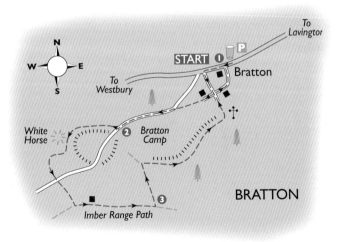

Guide to Wiltshire Pub Walks

2 Follow the path ahead along the edge of the hilltop, with fine views opening up across west **Wiltshire**. In 300 yards, continue to follow the path as it bears left to run above the **Westbury White Horse**; it then reaches a handgate. Beyond this handgate, climb some steps and turn right to walk across the hilltop, past some seats, to a topograph. Beyond the topograph, bear left, and walk across the hilltop to a gate and the road coming up from **Westbury**. Cross the road, and follow a grassy path to the right along to a beacon, before continuing for 150 yards to arrive at a gravelled byway on the left. Follow this byway for 200 yards up to the edge of the **Imber Ranges**; then bear left, and continue for 350 yards to **White Horse Farm**. Continue along the track for another 400 yards, before passing through a gate on the left to follow an enclosed bridleway.

3 Follow the bridleway for 250 yards, passing through a gateway along the way, until it emerges onto some open, bumpy ground. Continue along the path – it bears left for a few yards, and then right – to reach a gateway in 200 yards. Beyond this gateway, pass through a handgate on the right, and follow an enclosed path to another handgate. Beyond this gate, follow the line of a fence across the hilltop, high above **Combe Bottom**. In 250 yards, veer left – there is a marker – and follow a hillside path downhill towards **Bratton Church**. At the bottom of the slope, follow the path between some trees to reach a handgate at the end of the field. Continue along a hillside path through scrubland to a junction of paths. Turn left, and follow a path downhill past **Bratton Church**. Beyond the church, continue down a stepped path to a footbridge in the valley bottom, then walk uphill to reach a quiet back lane. Turn right; then, in 150 yards, turn left into the **Butts** by the **Oratory of St Giles**. Walk down to the B3098, and turn right to return to the **Duke**.

PLACES OF INTEREST NEARBY

Nearby **Trowbridge**, Wiltshire's county town, was once dubbed 'the Manchester of the South' on account of its textile history, which can be explored in the local museum (www.trowbridgemuseum.co.uk).

Downland view from the walk

15 Heytesbury
4 miles (6.4 km)

WALK HIGHLIGHTS
Dating back to the Saxon period, Heytesbury boasts a Norman church as well as the Hospital of St John and St Katharine, a Grade II listed 15th-century almshouse building. Flat and easy walking in the Wylye Valley from Heytesbury presents a quiet prelude to the dramatic hilltops above the village, where ancient earthworks and unimproved chalk grassland support some of the finest flora and fauna in the area.

THE PUB
The Red Lion www.redlionheytesbury.co.uk
☎ 01985 840315 **BA12 0EA**

THE WALK
1 Follow the pavement back to the **Cotley Hill roundabout**, and, walking anti-clockwise, take the third turning. (The first turning is the A36 to Southampton; the second is the B3414 to Warminster.) In 100 yards, just past a railway bridge, follow a footpath on the right down into a field. Head diagonally across the field to a gap in the hedgerow opposite; go through, and follow the left-hand edge of the following field to a gate, a stile and a lane by a red-brick cottage. Follow the lane ahead for 350

Guide to Wiltshire Pub Walks

HOW TO GET THERE AND PARKING: Follow the A36 to the Cotley Hill roundabout south of Warminster; take the turning into Heytesbury village. Drive along the High Street, and park on the roadside outside the Red Lion. **Postcode** BA12 0EA

MAP: OS Explorer 143 Warminster & Trowbridge. **Grid ref** 928426.

yards to a minor crossroads, ignoring one left turn along the way. At the crossroads, follow the track opposite – a waymarked footpath – for 400 yards to a junction.

2 Pass through the gateway opposite into a field, and follow a track to the left across a drainage ditch into the adjoining field. Turn right, and walk along the top edge of the field; 25 yards from the corner, pass through a gap on the right into the next field. Turn left, and follow the left-hand edge of the field for 350 yards to a barn and a bungalow. Cross the drive by the bungalow to a stile opposite, and walk across the field ahead – subdivided into paddocks – to join **Watery Lane** at its junction with the B3414. Turn left, and follow the lane – it becomes an enclosed path – for 350 yards, arriving at a footpath to **Bishopstrow Church** on the right. Follow this path, bearing left in 75 yards, to arrive at the church itself. Follow the path around the churchyard boundary wall to a handgate and a lane outside the church.

3 Ignoring the road on the left, follow the lane ahead between cottages, before continuing along a grassy track to the B3414 opposite **Old Stones**. Turn left; then, in 120 yards, turn right along the drive to **Home Farm**. Follow what becomes a track for ½ mile to a concrete army road, going straight over one crossroads along the way. Cross this road, enter the field opposite, and follow a grassy strip along the right-hand field boundary for 600 yards uphill to a junction below **Battlesbury Hill**. Turn right, and follow the left-hand edge of a field – this is the **Imber Range Perimeter Path** – to some steps and a road in the corner of the field, below **Middle Hill**. Turn right; then, in 20 yards, turn left through a gap in the bank onto the slopes of **Middle Hill**. Bear half-right uphill to reach the line of a fence on the hillside in 150 yards. Follow this fence for 300 yards around the southern slopes of **Middle Hill**. Just past a spinney, fork right downhill into the adjoining field. Head downhill across this field to a gap at the bottom and a lane below **Scratchbury Hill**.

4 Follow the lane ahead for 20 yards, before turning right and following a path uphill to a handgate at **Scratchbury Hillfort**. Turn left, and follow a path that veers to

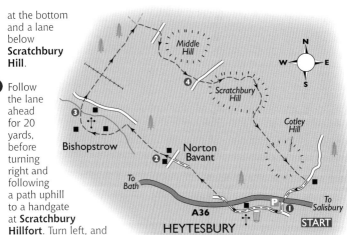

the right, away from the fence and up towards the lower rampart. Follow this rampart to the left, around the north and east of the hillside, to reach a handgate on the left in 600 yards. Turn left, and walk across a hilltop field to a handgate opposite. Follow the path across **Cotley Hill** for 350 yards to a handgate in the far-left corner of the field, before heading across an open hilltop to reach a tumulus in 250 yards. Pass to the left of this tumulus, then follow the path downhill to **Cotley Hill Woods**. Follow a track through the trees, before continuing downhill across an open field to an enclosed track and a lane. Turn right; in 300 yards, cross the A36, and follow the road opposite down to **Heytesbury High Street**. Turn right to return to the **Red Lion**.

PLACES OF INTEREST NEARBY
For detailed information about the area's rich history – both human and natural – visit **Warminster Museum** (www.warminstermuseum.org.uk).

Stonehenge

16 Stonehenge

6 miles (9.7 km)

WALK HIGHLIGHTS

This walk allows Britain's best-known ancient monument to be viewed from a distance, in its natural setting and far away from the hustle and bustle of the tourist traffic. Salisbury Plain is, after all, a landscape of open vistas and expansive views, something that cannot be appreciated from within the narrow confines of the stone circle itself. Along the way lie a number of important archaeological sites, including the Old and New King Barrows; the Avenue; and the Cursus, a linear enclosure that experts believe could have been the venue for chariot racing. This is truly a walk through the pages of ancient history!

THE PUB

The Stonehenge Inn & Carvery www.thestonehengeinn.co.uk
☎ 01722 790236 **SP4 8BN**

THE WALK

1 Walk along the road, passing the entrance to **Woodhenge** on the left; then pass a gate into the **Cuckoo Stone** enclosure. Walk across this

HOW TO GET THERE AND PARKING: Leave the A303 at Amesbury, and follow the A345 northwards towards Upavon and Devizes. In just under a mile, turn left into the Woodhenge parking area. **Postcode** SP4 7AR. For the pub, return to the A345 and turn left. In ½ mile, the Stonehenge Inn & Carvery is on the right, at the roundabout junction with the A3028. **Postcode** SP4 8BN

MAP: OS Explorer 130 Salisbury & Stonehenge. **Grid ref** 151433.

field to a second gate in its far-right corner. Bear left, and drop down to a track – the course of an old army railway line. Follow the track to the left. In 600 yards, and 100 yards before an electricity pylon, pass through a gap on the right to join a track. Follow this track – signposted to '**Old King Barrows and Stonehenge**' – for ¾ mile; then keep to the track as it bears right.

2 In 50 yards, turn left at a junction with another '**King Barrows**' sign. Follow this track for 350 yards – it bears left along the way – to reach

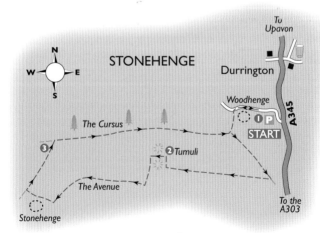

The Heel Stone standing at the entrance to the Stonehenge earthwork

an information board about the **Avenue** and a handgate on the right. Pass through this gateway, and walk across the field ahead, dropping downhill to reach a handgate in a fence in 600 yards. Beyond this gate, walk ahead to another information board; then bear left to walk uphill towards **Stonehenge**. On reaching a fence in front of this monument, turn right, and follow the line of fences for 300 yards to a gate and a track. Follow the track to the right for 600 yards to arrive at a point where the track has started to drop downhill and there are handgates on either side of the track.

3 Pass through the handgate on the right, and walk across to the far-left corner of the field ahead – this is now the course of the **Cursus**. Pass through a gate, cross a small paddock to another gate, and follow the left-hand edge of the next field for ½ mile to a gate and a track that leads to a crossroads. Follow the enclosed path opposite for ½ mile, until you reach a gap on the left by a **Ministry of Defence sign**. Turn left, and walk up to a handgate; enter the enclosure to retrace your steps from the beginning of the walk. Walk diagonally across the middle of the field to a gate and the road by the **Woodhenge** monument, before turning right to walk back to the parking area.

PLACES OF INTEREST NEARBY

For detailed information on the area, visit the **Amesbury History Centre**.

Stourhead in autumn

17 Stourhead
6 miles (9.7 km)

WALK HIGHLIGHTS
Henry Hoare, a wealthy London banker, erected the imposing Palladian mansion that is Stourhead House; he also surrounded it with grounds that are counted quite rightly among the most famous landscaped gardens in the world. Away from the splendours of this jewel in the National Trust's crown, the walk climbs up through Six Wells Bottom, passing St Peter's Pump and the source of the Stour, to reach King Alfred's Tower. From this monument, which marks the spot where Alfred and his army confronted the Danes, woodland paths through a remnant of Selwood Forest provide the return to Stourton and the delights of the Spread Eagle Inn.

THE PUB
The Spread Eagle Inn www.spreadeagleinn.com
☎ 01747 840587 **BA12 6QE**

Guide to Wiltshire Pub Walks

HOW TO GET THERE AND PARKING: The Stourhead Estate is signposted from the A303 at Mere. Park in the National Trust car park above the village. The Spread Eagle Inn is passed towards the end of the walk. **Postcode** BA12 6QF

MAP: OS Explorer 142 Shepton Mallet & Mendip Hills East. **Grid ref** 778340.

THE WALK

1 Pass through the **National Trust** entrance building at the bottom of the car park, and follow a path that winds its way downhill. (You do not need National Trust membership or to pay an entrance fee; just explain that you are walking around the estate, not visiting the house and grounds.) At a junction with a bridge leading to a walled garden ahead, follow the path to the right down to a road; opposite is an ornate entrance and a driveway leading to **Stourhead House**. Follow this driveway up to the house; bear right, crossing a cattle grid; and turn left on a path signposted to **King Alfred's Tower**. Beyond another cattle grid, veer left across parkland to an obelisk. Follow a track behind and to the left of

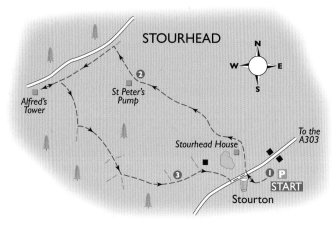

this obelisk down to a gate, before continuing downhill into **Six Wells Bottom**. Walk the length of this valley to reach **St Peter's Pump**, a monument that marks the source of the Stour.

❷ Pass to the right of **St Peter's Pump**, and climb uphill to reach a path on the hilltop known as the **Terrace**. Follow this path to the left to a gate, before continuing for ¾ mile to **King Alfred's Tower**. Having explored the tower area, retrace your steps for 250 yards back to a track with a barrier on the left; follow the track to the right into woodland. Ignoring one right turn, follow this path for ½ mile to a crossroads of tracks. Follow the path opposite downhill for 200 yards to the next crossroads of paths; here, turn left. Follow this path along the edge of the woodland, passing a barn early on, to reach a junction in 600 yards.

❸ Turn right, walking down to a gate at the edge of the woodland; then follow a footpath across the right-hand edge of a field to a gate. Continue along a track to reach a junction in 200 yards. Turn right – signposted to **Turner's Paddock** – and follow the path for 600 yards to a road on the edge of **Stourton**. Turn left. Having passed the entrance to **Stourhead Gardens** after 250 yards, veer right into a courtyard immediately past the **Spread Eagle Inn**. Turn left through the courtyard, pass under an archway, and follow the path ahead back up to the car park.

PLACES OF INTEREST NEARBY

Be sure to visit the historic town of **Mere**, just two miles from Stourhead. It has an excellent museum (www.meremuseum.org) that boasts over 7,000 artefacts.

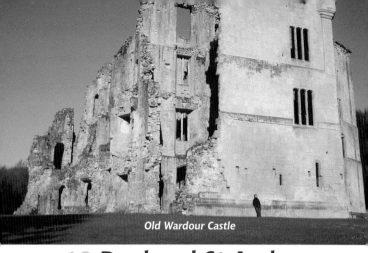

Old Wardour Castle

18 Donhead St Andrew

4 miles (6.4 km)

WALK HIGHLIGHTS

Deep in the wooded landscape of south Wiltshire, the romantic ruin of Old Wardour Castle stands in a secluded lakeside setting, a victim of a Civil War ransacking. Nearby is New Wardour Castle – more of a stately home than a fortification. Away from these historic masterpieces, this delightful walk explores open hillsides and shady woodland in a special – yet little-visited – corner of Wiltshire.

THE PUB

The Forester www.theforesterdonheadstandrew.co.uk
☎ 01747 828038 **SP7 9EE**

THE WALK

❶ Walk back up to the main road; turn left towards the **Forester**. Continue for 100 yards to a junction; take the right fork, signposted to **Salisbury**. Continue for 350 yards to a minor crossroads; follow the cul-de-sac lane opposite. Continue for 200 yards to a stile and a gate on the left;

HOW TO GET THERE AND PARKING: Donhead St Andrew is off the A30, a few miles east of Shaftesbury. At a minor crossroads a mile east of Ludwell, where a signpost south indicates Berwick St John, take the unmarked lane opposite, then take the first left to park roadside by St Andrew's church. For the Forester, instead of turning off to the church, keep going on the unmarked lane until you reach the pub on your right. However, there is very little parking outside. **Postcode** SP7 9EB

MAP: OS Explorer 118 Shaftesbury & Cranborne Chase. **Grid ref**

cross the stile, and walk down the right-hand end of a paddock to a gate and a stile at the entrance to **Park Copse**. Beyond this gate, follow the woodland path ahead for 200 yards to a gate and an open field above **Park Gate Farm**. Walk down the right-hand side of this field to cross a stile in the bottom corner. Turn left and almost immediately right to follow a waymarked path through the farmyard. Pass through a handgate on the far side, and follow an enclosed path – with the farmhouse behind the hedge on the left – to the next handgate.

2 Enter an open field, and follow the right-hand boundary for 600 yards to a gate and a stile in the corner. In the next field, walk to the middle of the opposite boundary – initially hidden in a dip – and pass through a gateway. Head uphill to a stile in the top boundary. Cross a concrete drive and a stile opposite; head uphill in the next field to cross a stile in the boundary at the left-hand end of a belt of trees. Follow a woodland path to emerge by **Wardour Court**; pass by on the right, and follow a clearly marked grassy path to a junction by a lodge. Turn right, and follow a path to the parking area in front of **New Wardour Castle**; at the far side, bear half-left away from the house along a track. After 50 yards, cross a stile on the right into an open field; follow the path across this field towards **Ark Farm**. On the far side, cross a stile, join a track, and turn left. Continue along this track through **Ark Farm** and onto a junction by the parking area for **Old Wardour Castle**.

3 Turn right, and follow the lane that runs below the wall of the ruined castle. Keep to this path beyond the castle; it bears right to climb above the southern shore of the lake. In 300 yards, ignore a track to **Ark Farm** on the right, keeping to the main track. In 100 yards, keep right at a fork; continue along the track until it ends at an open field. Follow the right-hand field boundary down to a gate in the bottom corner. Continue along a woodland path – with **Pale Park Pond** on the left – to the next gate; then head uphill through the field to a gate and a stile at the entrance to **Wardour Wood**. Walk ahead to a junction, turn right, and follow the waymarked **Wessex Ridgeway** for 250 yards to a gate exiting the woodland. Continue along the track for 350 yards, passing **Pile Oak Lodge**, to return to the crossroads. Follow the lane ahead downhill into **Donhead St Andrew**, turning left at the next junction to return to the **Forester**.

PLACES OF INTEREST NEARBY

Take time to visit the historic market town of **Shaftesbury** (www. shaftesburytourism.co.uk).

Groveley Wood

19 Great Wishford

5 miles (8 km)

WALK HIGHLIGHTS

This relaxing walk begins in the attractive village of Great Wishford, lying in the Wylye Valley between Warminster and Salisbury, and ascends onto the wooded hills to the south-west, deep into the ancient forest of Grovely Wood. Come this way on May 29th, Oak Apple Day, and you will find the locals enacting an ancient custom known as the Grovely Forest Rights. This annual ceremony is when the residents of Great Wishford claim their right to collect 'all kinde of deade snapping woode, boughs and stickes' from the local forest. An oak bough is lopped, decked in ribbons and carried ceremonially to Great Wishford Church, where it is hung from the tower.

THE PUB

The Royal Oak www.royaloakgreatwishford.com
☎ 01722 790613 **SP2 0PD**

Guide to Wiltshire Pub Walks

HOW TO GET THERE AND PARKING: Leave the A36 at Stoford, three miles north of Wilton, and follow an unclassified road signposted to Great Wishford. On entering the village, drive past the church and the village school, and park in the vicinity of the Royal Oak. **Postcode** SP2 0PD

MAP: OS Explorer 130 Salisbury & Stonehenge. **Grid ref** 079355.

THE WALK

1 Walk under the railway bridge by the **Royal Oak**, and follow a quiet lane for just over a mile to the entrance to **Grovely Wood**. Where the road ends at the entrance to the woodland, continue, following a track uphill. In ¾ mile, at a crossroads, carry straight on. In another 350 yards,

The Royal Oak

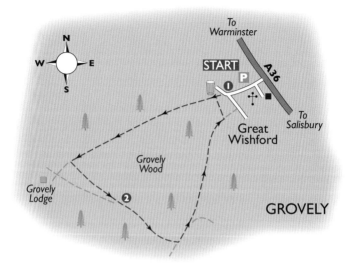

shortly before a junction on the edge of the woodland, follow a footpath on the left – there is a waymark on a telegraph pole on the right.

2 In ¼ mile, join a broad track; follow this track beyond a barrier for ¾ mile to a crossroads with a bridleway sign on a tree on the right. Turn left to follow this bridleway, ignoring a grassy path that veers off on the right in 300 yards. Keep to the bridleway – it emerges from the woodland onto open downland – for just over a mile to arrive at a barrier on the edge of **Great Wishford**. Beyond the barrier, follow a track on the left to return to a junction with the road. Turn right, pass under the railway bridge once again, and return to the **Royal Oak**.

PLACES OF INTEREST NEARBY
Wilton Shopping Village (www.wiltonshoppingvillage.co.uk) is housed in part of the former Wilton Carpet Factory complex, which dates back to 1710.

20 **Broad Chalke**

6½ miles (10.5 km)

WALK HIGHLIGHTS

Broad Chalke lies west of Salisbury, deep in the heart of the Ebble Valley. The Ebble is one of the five rivers that converge on the city, in this case the river having its confluence with the Avon in the water meadows to the south of the cathedral. All around the village lies the archetypal chalk downland – with expansive views and big skies at every turn – that forms the central focus of this walk. There is also a section of the Old Shaftesbury Drove, a medieval track running from Shaftesbury to Salisbury; as its name suggests, it was used for moving livestock between the two markets on foot.

THE PUB

The Queen's Head www.queensheadbroadchalke.co.uk
☎ 01722 780344 **SP5 5EN**

THE WALK

1 With your back to the pub, follow the road to the right around a

HOW TO GET THERE AND PARKING: Leave the A30 just west of Fovant, a village that lies between Shaftesbury and Wilton, and follow the well-signposted road into Broad Chalke. Park on the roadside in the vicinity of the Queen's Head and the Chalke Valley Stores. **Postcode** SP5 5EN

MAP: OS Explorer 130 Salisbury & Stonehenge. **Grid ref** 039256.

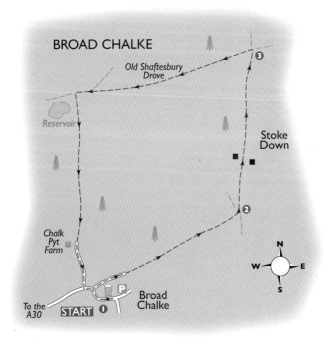

right-hand bend before taking the first right in 100 yards – a cul-de-sac signposted to the **Queen's Head** car park. Follow this lane along to where it ends by a thatched cottage; continue along the path that runs to the left of this property. In 120 yards, where the path emerges into the corner of an open field, walk ahead a few paces and continue, following the course of the path between hedgerows at the top of arable fields. In ½ mile, where the path reaches the corner of a field and a belt of trees, turn right into the adjoining field, and follow a path down to a concrete farm road.

② Turn left, and follow this road for 600 yards to a collection of farm buildings. Continue for ½ mile before veering right onto a grassy path running alongside the field boundary on the right. (Do not follow the track that runs inside the field itself, parallel to the correct path.) In 350 yards, keep to the path as it bears right, away from the field, to pass through some woodland; in 50 yards, it emerges into an arable field. Walk diagonally across the middle of this field; a few isolated trees mark the course of a bridleway. On the far side of the field, keep walking in the same direction through some woodland, ignoring side turns, until the bridleway joins a farm road after 250 yards. Follow this road up to the junction, where it meets the track known as the **Old Shaftesbury Drove**.

③ Turn left, and follow the **Old Shaftesbury Drove** for just under two miles to a left turn, immediately beyond which is a reservoir hidden in the trees. Turn left, and follow a track for 1½ miles down to **Chalke Pyt Farm**. Continue past the farm buildings down to the road in **Broad Chalke**. Walk ahead to pass the cul-de-sac on the left – the route from the outset – and keep to the road as it bears left to bring you back to the pub.

PLACES OF INTEREST NEARBY

Housed in a former chapel, **Chalke Valley Stores** in Broad Chalke (www.chalkevalleystores.co.uk) has won national acclaim as one of the country's best community shops.